Words, Thoughts, Observations

18 / 100

J. R. Easton

Words, Thoughts, Observations

J R Easton

Printed by Biddles Books, Kings Lynn, Norfolk PE32 1SF

1st Edition 2020

The Author

J. R. Easton

My first poem was written for a school magazine in the CND days of the early 80s and was prompted by the fear I felt due to the intensity of the Cold War. I remember discussing the issues with the then Labour Party leader, Michael Foot when he visited the school.

Having left school in 1983 with little by way of qualifications, and completely obsessed with Gary Numan, I worked under the Government's Youth Training Scheme at a Cash and Carry in Radcliffe, Bury.

Always harbouring an ambition to become a policeman, in April 1989, I started a career that spanned just over 30 years. I retired in 2019.

Despite the experience of the first poem, for whatever reason, I did not write again until around 2015 when a copy of the School Magazine, posted on social media, reminded me of the poem that I had written back in the day.

I decided to write a poem to mark an anniversary, which in turn lead to several other family poems being written.

These kindled a sense of creative achievement which prompted me to diversify.

Written throughout 2019 and in particular, during the 2020 Lockdown, the 80 poems contained in this book are the result.

Did I mention Gary Numan? Listen to Replicas.

For Mum, Dad,
Michelle,
Heather, James and Alexander

X X
X
X X X

Contents

This book is in 5 sections:

30 years, 3 months and 15 days in 'The Job'

Covid 19

Our Prison

Hollins Vale

Others

30 Years, 3 Months, 15 Days in The Job

So many great colleagues,
dealing with the worst that society could throw at us.
It was an honour.

When I joined

I joined 'The Job', in April 89
I reflect, and look back, such a bygone time
trained for 14 sunny weeks at Bruche
a defining time that ended my youth

Rent Allowance, Dental costs and Prescriptions
benefits we lost despite protestations
we earned £10,500 a year
some Nicks had a bar where you could get a late beer

Each Division had a canteen
where you could get your Refs
to protect ourselves, we had wooden 'staffs'
we didn't have body armour, CS or Tazers
we had woollen trousers, and tunics, like blazers

The ashtrays in CID were stolen from pubs
we had an LIO, which is now called 'The HUB'
the intelligence system was in Lever Arch Files
and a card index system
that must have stretched miles

All statements and files were handwritten by you
checked by the Sergeant, you hoped it'd get through
mistakes were highlighted, by a thick red line
not bullying... Development, you got it right next time

We went out 'as a Relief' on Thursday before nights
for a beer and a laugh, and to put the wrongs, right
no grievance procedure, you just did as you were told
we went out walking, in the rain and the cold

We'd walk, with our legs, around our beat
we had brew stops, we'd visit, to rest our feet
Probationers went out, and got wet, in the rain
4 quick changeovers each month, scrambled your brain

You always knew, that your scrote was a thief
if he kicked off on arrest and demanded a 'Brief'
we gave evidence in trials, every month at Crown Court
each division had its own back office support

And every Division has its own Chief Super'
fingerprints were taken, with ink, on paper
no High-Vis jackets or mobile phones
no Air Support, Helicopters or drones

Every Division had its own shift pattern
and don't even think of going out with no hat on
your application for Leave, may well get refused
the division had five computers that we couldn't use

Every Relief... was self-sufficient,
our own Traffic, Dogs, Custody and Comms' contingent
dedicated Comms' staff who had once worked the same streets
and knew the Division, and the people you'd meet

The Bosses wore white
the Bobbies, blue shirts
the ladies were 'Policewomen'
issued with handbags and skirts

The girls got a 'sexist' allowance for tights
we had D Reg Mini Metros, and you hear this right
Panda Cars didn't have "Blues" or "Twos"
we pressed our pants and we bulled our shoes

If you locked up, you'd stay on, to complete the task
a request to come in late?... You dare not ask
but your overtime was paid, no 'half hour for the Queen'
if the 'Bail Bunny' said no, then your prisoner 'stayed in'

So, if you finished at 3, you'd be back on at 7
you could get your head down when you had Refs at eleven
standards were important, there's no denying
whenever you finished, your shirt needed ironing

A crime with no prisoner, came back every time
the DCI's Question... 'Where's the evidence of crime?'
a window smashed, a burglar around
Minor Damage Report, value £24

RTCs were RTAs
Giros, reported, stolen on Thursdays
on every shift, we had plenty of Cops
no need for cardboard cut-outs in shops

Every locker... had been forced at some time
people got arrested for committing crime
no 'Necessity for arrest', Just "You're nicked, mate"
interviews were handwritten on 808s

You weren't a 'Student Officer', you were 'in your Probation'
we had cops parading on at every station
your Sergeant or Inspector would 'show you a visit'
secondments secured to the Plain Clothes Unit,

A prosecution file, might just be a 330
to check Insurance or Licence, we'd issue a HORTi
a Summons Green Card, 'Fail to Produce at the scene'
blow in the bag until the crystals turn green

A community centre that was once Cheetham Nick
Grey Mare Lane is a film set, Plant Hill, derelict
Collyhurst is demolished, Chester House too
memories of a time when I worked with you.

Pressing the button

I'm dressed like a cop
But I don't know what to do
The new Sprog on the Block
I haven't got a clue
Today's first objective
Just set for me
To check out a vehicle on the PNC
Over the radio
The whole Division can hear
Mind and mouth
Affected by fear
My Tutor, Stella,
Suggests I rehearse
The prospect leaves me
Stuttering with nerves
The button I must press
Feels like a detonator
The increasing stress
As I wait for the Radio Operator

"6198, to the PNC"
"Go ahead 6198, a vehicle or body?"

Hesitation, as I rehearse my lines

My mouth has gone dry, but Stella says I'll be fine
The Phonetic Alphabetic must not be forgotten
The Division tunes in as I press on the button...

"A vehicle please,
On Cheetham Hill Road"

So far so good
My message flowed

"Go ahead with the details..."

Increasingly confident

Alpha
2 6 7
Juliet...

Norman,

Elephant

BOOM!

The Custody Sergeant

A young PC's first solo arrest
Under pressure, *I've got to pass this test*
The Custody Sergeant, a Supreme Being

A person who seems to know everything
Totally 'on it', constantly assessing
A deity of the Cops it seems

I cringe when *he's* on, it adds to my ordeal
When I lock up late and stay on to deal
He seems so unhelpful and rude

I've been on 15 hours, I'm starting to stink,
I'm in need of a shower and gagging for a drink
And it's been ages since I had any food

This growling Sergeant who never smiles
And always wants to check my files
I feel that I have to impress him

But he never gives credit, or so it seems
He runs Custody with a tight regime
He's really grumpy and intimidating

I cross every I, and dot every T
My nerves have got the better of me
I start again, I've got to get it right

I check the fine detail, every page, completely
But he still finds errors that I didn't see
And now it's approaching midnight

The offence investigated, proved and admitted
The file eventually, signed and submitted
The prisoner charged, bedded down and remanded

I'm back on at seven, in 6 hours' time
Hungry and filthy, with Custody grime
I need a lift to my Nick, and I'm stranded

Twelve years later and that Sergeant is me
Grumpy and stressed running Custody
I've upset a young cop doing her best

My excuse, I'm under pressure with 34 cells
There are doors being banged and nasty smells
I could have helped her, but now she's distressed.

Quick Change Over

I should have finished at 11
But I've only just got home
I'm back in work at 7
And it's half past One

I've had a quick shower
Now I'm lying in my bed
I've got to try and stop thinking
The jobs are buzzing around my head

I close my eyes, I've got to sleep
My body is so tired
My mind debriefing every job
I'm feeling totally wired

It's 230 am, I'm up at 6
But as yet I've hardly slept
My mind's creating a 'To-Do' list
With all the jobs unchecked

By 3am they're prioritised
And I hope I can now get some rest
But my mind is preparing a plan of attack
And soon it'll be time to get dressed

4am, I've nodded off
I can finally get some sleep
In just a couple of hours
The alarm clock will start to beep

At 545 I wake in a panic
I mustn't oversleep
These 15 minutes of rest, now lost
Quick-Changeovers make me weep

A day shift awaits, 'To-Do' list ignored
By Refs I'm starting to tire
I'll finish at 3, fall asleep on the settee
And catch up with the sleep I require.

The Panda Car

Sunday morning Vehicle Checks
Damage found, What the heck?
Mileage missed - Logbook incomplete
It's done 200000 miles
Around local streets

It's 4 years old
But it's never been frozen
No matter how cold
The interior condition?

It's a total disgrace
... Check the brakes
And in the boot
An empty box of cakes

Or empty bottles of Coke
Best check the tyres
In the First Aid Kit
Is a pair of plyers

And a screwdriver
And an apple core
The rear brake light
Needs replacing once more

The Fire Extinguisher?
There isn't one
The Jack and Brace?
Both have gone

The Windscreen Washers:
Dry as a bone
Blues and Twos
Work when turned on

So that's all-in order
For another week
And if you defect it
You're walking the streets.

Next of Kin

Details over the radio
Your name and address
My job: to pass a message
To deliver distress

I compose myself
As I make my way
Practising the words
That I might say

It gets no easier
Though I've done it before
I compose myself
Then knock on the door

I see you approach
Through frosted glass
Your life about to change
Due to the message I'll pass

The shock on your face
Changes to fear
Seeing me in this place
You realise why I'm here

You hope it's something else
As our worlds collide
But you know the truth
"Can I come inside?"

You offer me tea
Trying to delay
Not wanting to hear
What I have to say

"Would you like to sit down?
I have some bad news."
You wonder which loved one
You're about to lose

I say the words
Who, how and where
Your eyes drop to the floor
As you sit in the chair

I'm looking for a sign
That you'll be alright
And search for a friend
Who can come here tonight

This irreversible change
That I've brought to your life
The sudden numbness
From normal to strife

The unfillable void
The sense of grief
I make you a tea
Our acquaintance is brief

Then a knock at the door
That friend has come around
Your time to grieve
The moment, profound

I take my leave, and close the door
In the car I reflect, we've not met before
But you'll never forget my knock on your door
The one time we met, the day I imparted
News of a loved one
Now sadly departed

"6198, a result when you're ready."
To Comms, over the air,
*"Death message passed, next of kin
are informed and are aware."*

"6198, thanks for that, I've got a domestic,
it's just come in
a child has phoned via 999
saying mum and dad are fighting."

Domestic

I'm 23 years old
and I am here to advise
How you two
in your 40s
ought to live your lives
the difficulties you face
the medication you use
the stress of your circumstances
blowing your fuse
the drunken arguments
the impact on your children
your family in crisis
the conditions they live in
my limited experience
at work and in life
but you're under arrest
for assaulting your wife
intoxicated domestic
my only constraint
early next week
she'll retract her complaint
and then next Sunday evening
we'll do it all again
this cycle of chaos
destruction and pain.

Child Killer

As you watched the football
A child cried
You took her from her cot

She needed a parent
At your hand, she died
Defenceless little tot

An act that now
can't be undone
You're responsible for her death

You're a child killing murderer
Until your final breath.

Crown Court

Middle of a set of nights
1030 in the morning
Someone ringing the doorbell
Wakes me whilst I'm snoring
A Police Car is parked outside
And a Cop is knocking on
I rush downstairs
In a panic, to find out what's going on...

"You dealt with a suicide
The deceased is due in Court
The Judge won't stay the case today
Until evidence is brought
By someone who has seen the body
And can confirm the ID"

Other than family members
It seems that man is me.

Up and dressed with just 2 hours sleep,
When I should be in my bed
I'm up and out and on my way
to Manchester Crown instead

I get to Court and speak to the Clerk
He says that I'm on next
The Prosecutor has the details
And will lead me through the facts

In 'The Box' I take the Oath,
And state my Name and Rank
And that a Paramedic
Had confirmed his life extinct

I confirm the defendant's sister
Attended the Mortuary
And identified the deceased
As her brother, the defendant, to me

I was only in the Court
For two minutes,
maybe three
And in that time
The Judge didn't even speak or look at me.

So I'm off to home
No longer tired
But later, I'll be shattered
The Court got to bin another case
And that's all that really mattered.

Murderer

Your life carries on
Whilst another, is gone
Your actions ended a life
He took a last breath
You caused his death
A family wrecked with strife

All the lies, in mitigation
Your defence exculpation
A difficult upbringing is blamed
A plea to manslaughter
A fatherless daughter
You'll soon be released, yet again

Was true justice served?
By a sentence of 4 years
Out in 12 months due to your remand
Your conscience seems clear
The cost of your actions, so dear
An innocent man died at your hand

I'm shocked now to see
How nonchalantly
You've behaved, since you were released
The family still grieves
You continue to thieve
Indifferent to the life now deceased.

Rachel Street

New probationers arrived on Division
An itinerary by way of an introduction
To the jobs and the area, where we'd work

There is no doubt, that Death walks these streets
It's best that we're prepared, else when on our Beats
We might see something, nasty, then shirk

I'd never seen a dead body before
The morning I walked through the door
Of the Rachel Street Mortuary

I have a strong natural aversion
But also sensed voyeuristic fascination
With the things I was destined to see

I was relieved, nonetheless, to hear
the post-mortems had already been done
The Attendant suggested, with no hint of irony
that we had 'Missed all the fun'

And I wondered, to myself...

...who applies
to be a Mortuary Attendant?
A perfect role
if you like to work alone
with quiet people and disinfectant

But in the fridge,
he had three he'd 'made earlier'
Actual dead bodies
that made my toes curlier

He proudly got them out for us to see
Examined, and now at peace
An old man, an old lady
And a baby
Sewn up, and ready for release

Things that I
now cannot un-see
Like the clinical efficiency
Of the post-mortem room

A processing plant
for a human cadaver
Stark, dark, functional and macabre
A place of darkness and doom.

A Jumper

On a November morning a body is found
At the foot of the flats
Face down on the ground
A lad in his twenties
Who'd been there for hours
Before we got a call from a girl in this tower
She'd heard a noise
But it was dark at the time
She'd looked out again at twenty to nine
And then she saw him
Lying below
And looked up and noticed
An open window
On the 14th floor
Locked from the inside
We'll never know, the turmoil in his life
That caused such sorrow
Or how sad at that time
Who did he think about?
As he tried to decide?
How long did he sit there?
What swayed his mind?
As he'd climbed out...
That peace he would find.
And as he fell, was he sure?
That this, was what he wanted?
A sorrowful scene, police tape secured,
A grieving family haunted.

Heart Shaped Scar

On patrol, but off my beat
A car is parked, on a dodgy street
Little signs I notice, to me it is clear
This car is stolen, and it shouldn't be here.

I pull alongside, in my liveried van
And get out, wearing uniform, a policeman
As I notice the vehicle is insecure
I hear a noise, a closing door.

But when the door was opened, a dog was pushed out
A bull terrier, with lots of teeth in his snout
Intended to intimidate, but I wasn't moved
I noticed the chassis number had been removed

A back up call, as the threat is sensed...

And then it began.

My life about to change
As the door reopened, he charged into range
At first, I thought he was joking,
I couldn't make out what he said
Then shock as I realised, I'd been punched to the head.

Again and again, disoriented, confused
I raised my guard, my head is bruised
I landed a punch as I start to fight back
The dog was set to, by an order to attack.

Slow motion,
as I assess this developing situation.
His punches still land, but there's a new sensation
My body suffers elsewhere, as I'm punched again
There's a dog on my leg, and significant pain.

A further assessment, whilst I'm still on my feet
Do I fight him, or the dog? Both, I can't defeat
I concentrate on the dog, as they continue to attack
I prise open his mouth, but the dog bounces back.

I know I'm overwhelmed, as the teeth lock again
A crushing and tearing kind of pain
The punches don't hurt, but I sense trauma from my thigh
BANG! another punch lands as I'm hit in the eye.

I retreat, cover my head and go to the ground
The dog's on my leg, as I'm dragged around
Whilst a mother and child, walk to school unperturbed
A normal Thursday morning in this neighbourhood?

As I curl up and protect as best I can
An accomplice came out and smashed up my van
As the sirens approach, he ran back in through the door
My battle is lost, I pass out on the floor.

Then done... It was over, that was it.
So much had happened in just one minute
From getting out of the van, to unconscious on the floor
The difficulties will be experienced for 2 decades and more.

A guy from the Direct Works helped me up to my feet
My uniform dishevelled, as my mates arrive in the street
A warmth on my leg, drains down from my thigh
My face swollen and a cut to my eye.

To Hospital.
The nurses, recognised my distress
Bruised, bloodied, and also upset, I confess
Clothing removed, the first time that I see
The wounds to my leg, did it eat part of me?

Injected, treated, cleaned, injuries dressed
Upset, confused, pretty distressed
How did this happen? What should I have done?
If I'd been better prepared, I could have won.

The hole in my leg, will form a heart-shaped scar
This dog bite's not stitched, the risk of infection is far...
...too great, and if infected, it would need 'invasive treatment'
So the scars are left to form, as a tormentor, they're
permanent.

I hear on the radio, that the news has broken
'A Police Officer's in hospital...' my Mum will be shaken
I give her a call, before she discovers the truth
That I am the cop, talked about on the news.

And then home.
Sore, shocked, angry, confused
What? Why? Totally bemused
Time off work, unable to walk
The long-term injury, I was unable to talk.

Physical injuries healed after a while
The real blow delivered, after a 2-week trial
Where a barrister conspired to his perjured defence
This caused my injury, and significant offence.

A dishonest barrister
lead this farce in Crown Court
A regular defender, of my assailant, who sought
To influence the jury
who in turn failed to convict
Another assault, via an unjust verdict.

Career and spirit, affected for years
Desperate for help, but prevented by fears
That to ask for help, would suggest inadequacy
Desperate that someone would notice and help me.

He served years 'inside' for other indiscretions
The Court's failure fuelled a crushing depression
The sense of injustice, I wanted to secure
A 'right' for the 'wrong', that happened in Court Number 4.

Whenever he was out, I sought opportunity
I stayed within the law, but I wanted him to pay
Then a chance 'in the shadows', taken and assured
A significant sentence, my justice secured.

The Living Dead

Opportunity stolen by proxy thieves
Families destroyed
So many empty lives
Their dreams... now void
One terrible choice
A pathway chosen
With a consequence.
A lesson learned
There seems no way back
Unable to return
Dependant on Smack
The only desire
To get another bag
A whole life's fire
Extinguished by Scag
The parental fear
A critical frown
'Your kid's on gear' 'Your kid's on brown'
The stolen possessions
The sunken eyes
The family shame
The deceit and lies
Can't find a vein
The stolen trust
A rattlin' wreck
Needles... Must.
A phone call... "Have you got?"
A once capable child, now destined to rot

A pain in the leg, a DVT?
A young girl's loss of dignity
The rotten teeth
'Have you got a pin?'
Sharing 'works'
Desperately thin
A day spent 'graftin'
Things to steal
A filter and citric
A recipe for a 'meal'
That you're cooking up
In a spoon for a pan
Or foil and a flame
To chase the dragon
Using a lighter
Boiling the mix
Shooting up into an ulcer
Another £10 fix
To the Needle Exchange
For a Safety Pack
Your Mam's had enough
She's on your back
Alone in the world
You're on the street
A social circle limited
To other zombies that you meet
A Bag Head, a Bag Rat
With a DVT
Hepatitis, Aids or HIV.

In the Shadows

Spiders,
Weaving webs,
A trap set,
Barbed hooks,
Heavily baited,
To attract you.
Seeing is believing.
Believing what you want to believe,
Infiltrating...
Those hooks,
Psychologically tailored,
To your motivations,
Temptation,
Weaknesses exposed,
Penetrating,
Deeply,
Into the nature of your being,
It takes time,
Patiently waiting,
In the shadows,
The deceit,
The betrayal,
Waiting,
For you to respond,
In the way that you do,
Inevitably.

Promotion

I worked for that rank
Acting and Assessment
I stressed more than I needed

But the 3 Silver Chevrons
On my new tunic
Look so good it must be conceded.

A supervisor now
My own Relief
Staff to be directed and managed

A team to build
Standards instilled
Developed, helped and encouraged.

Drink Driver

A vehicle check
No insurance held
MOT expired

The car pulled over
Stinking of beer
Fail to provide when required

Details recorded
Rights and Entitlements
Detention authorised

I explain the position
You need to provide a breath specimen
You need to be breathalysed

You signed the forms
You spoke to a solicitor
To help you understand

If it's 'Under' you'll be released
This is your last chance
If it's 'Over' you'll be Banned

"One continuous breath
Until I say STOP"
It's not a good idea to refuse

"Don't suck, just blow"
The machine will know
It's the lower of 2 readings we'll use

"Keep going, Keep going
Keep going, Stop!
The first of two samples secured

The process repeated
The Breathalyser completed
A tense wait for the readings, endured

A lower reading of 126
The limit is 35
You are nearly 4 times over

"I'm going to lose my job
I need my licence for work"
A point you ignored when you drove

Fingerprints, Photo and DNA
Then to a cell
whilst the file's completed

Charged and released
On bail to the Court
A process so often repeated.

Detention Authorised

Arrested, resisting
Violent and spitting
Handcuffed and restrained

An officer bleeding
Bitten on her arm
An injury on duty sustained

Brought into custody
Kicking and screaming
Circumstances outlined

Details refused
Offensive and crude
Rights and Entitlements unsigned

Reason for arrest?
"Affray and assault"
Your identity revealed by Livescan

"And you can throw on a criminal damage, Sarge,
Coz he's pissed in the back of the van."

Detention authorised
I try to get you booked in
And get you Risk Assessed

"I want a Brief, I want a phone call,
I know my rights"
"I want to press charges, unlawful arrest"

"I pay your wages
I want to make a complaint"
I want to see an Inspector"

You are agitated and aggressive
Uncooperative
"Put all your property on the counter"

A PNC Check
on the Livescan details
You are wanted all over the country

A robbery in Yorkshire
Another in Merseyside
A burglary in GMP

A series of Drive Offs
A Locate Trace
And a TWOC in Devon and Cornwall

Fail to Appear
At Preston Crown Court
And to top it, a Prison Recall.

A Cop in Custody

I ask for your name,
Date of Birth, home address
I've outlined the reasons
For your arrest
I've explained why your detention
Has been authorised
But I notice a flicker
As I look in your eyes
You're familiar with this process
But you're shown as 'Not Known'
Then I understand
You are one of our own.

A domestic
Drink Driving
Minor public order
The usual reasons
That a Cop gets in bother
A check of your wallet
My suspicion confirmed
A Police Warrant Card
You are recently affirmed
Drink Drive on this occasion
Too much red wine
An uncomfortable situation
Your career on the line

The Inspector's informed
And the Duty Silver
Complaints and Discipline
Are making their way over

The breathalyser process
Followed to a 'T'
Your only hope
A reading under fifty

It doesn't take long
The lowest is 78
Twice over the legal limit
Resigned to your fate
Charged and Bailed
Suspension in due course
An appointment with the Chief
Then dismissed from the Force.

Tony, Gordon, David, Theresa and Boris

Year after year
Different administrations
Labour, Conservative, pander 'The Press'
Change this, adjust that
New working conditions
Their aim each time, is more for less

Years of 'Know How'
Swept aside at what harm?
Developed and passed over generations
Decades of stability
Understanding and calm
Sacrificed to boost your career aspirations

Sensational politics
Promotion at risk
'Volume Crime', our bread and butter
Home Office priorities
That we already address
Weaponised against us, the Service stutters

The media
Politicise, methods that work
Tazers, ASBOs, Horses and Dogs
'Controversial' Tactics
like Stop and Search
Basic policing for neighbourhoods

Our society Is a violent place
Whilst we're expected to be a 'service'
A 'Spit Hood'? Or, spat at, in the face
Our Finest don't deserve this

Politicians, though
Are in a privileged position
A family wedding wiped out by a drone missile
Their mistakes, excused
Immune from prosecution
Whilst a retired Chief Super stands trial

Much crime is driven, by greed and drugs
Detections magnify the failings
Resources are moved to other thugs
The Courts are no longer jailing

Repeat offenders, continue to offend
Our Girls and Boys can't cope
Their numbers slashed to fund austerity
There's really little hope

Successive, Governments, seem intent
To provide offenders with help and support
Whilst Victims are dismissed
No effective deterrent, the failings of our Courts

So, you've, crafted the service,
That you deserve, our failings, forced by you,
Instead you suggest that we're 'Crying Wolf',
The responsibility lies with you.

30 Years, 3 Months, 15 Days

An appointment in January 1958,
Set a path that probably sealed my fate,
My Dad, B23, joins the Manchester Force,
From Constable to Chief Super, my inspiration of course.

At a Radcliffe Cash and Carry, lessons were learned,
Hard physical graft, but very little earned,
A lifeline grabbed, I start my career,
An oath is sworn, 'Without favour, nor fear'.

Five years to the day, since they killed Yvonne Fletcher,
Her body recovered on an ambulance stretcher,
A political murder, outside the Libyan Embassy,
The police are just pawns in a prime ministry.

Two days after Hillsborough, my career began,
On the 17th April, I became a policeman,
Twenty-two years old, when I begin my time,
At Sedgley Park and Bruche, Intake 3 of 89.

August '89, To GMP's B Division,
" *What if Strangeways 'went up'?*" was Wally Elder's question,
Eddie Forshaw, overlooks as the Training Sergeant,
Stella Jones my tutor, plots my development.

B relief on 'The B', led by Inspector Mary Bee,
Sgts Hitchen, Nobby Clarke and Norman Cassidy,
Pete Giles and Alan Johnson followed soon from 'The A',
Standards were set that are followed to this day.

From Starmoor Walk, Cheetham, an inadequate chap,
Stole his own boiler, and weighed it in as scrap,
Flooding his neighbours at 8, 6, 4 and 2,
Mr Smith, my first arrest, my memory of you.

Thomas Joseph Gilligan, a 'vagrant' infested with lice,
Did any other officer, arrest this man twice?
First theft by finding, then released to ensure,
That I'd get the warrant and have to arrest him once more.

A shooting at Birch Services, on the 14th of September,
'Officers down', their names I remember,
A suspect on a motorbike, filling up with fuel,
Unarmed officers shot, an act so cruel.

The Inspector is murdered, his Sergeant survives,
The bullet stopped by his pocketbook, saving his life,
I'm honoured to be on Hospital Watch guarding Sergeant Jim,
ACC Malcolm George visits whilst I look after him.

Strangeways 'went up', it was no April Fool,
Wally's premonition, 8 months later, came true,
For 25 days, we're the focus of the World,
The prison destroyed as the story unfurled.

Rest Day 'Containers' at Grey Mare Lane or Plant Hill,
A couple each month earns plenty of 'Till',
Sex offenders, child killers, *'Boss, can I have a shower?'*,
Dirty protests, cell searches, what a way to spend 12 hours.

February 91, at the old Penny Black,
A gangster is murdered, shot in the back,
Face down and lifeless, his hands told a story,
Fingers curled into the soil, the scene I found was gory.

A man in a wheelchair, tries to cause a collision,
Seeking more compensation, to fund his alcohol addiction,
Pushing himself into the road, as the lights turn to green,
Sean Devine, one of the saddest cases, that I've ever seen

From Ashton Old Road, I turned into Victoria Street,
I stopped... aghast and looked up, twenty feet,
The thing I saw provoked a nervous laugh,
A real, full size, adult male, Giraffe.

So I asked myself, as it crossed an Openshaw road,
"Is this real?" but it simply strode,
From kerb to kerb, as I sat waiting in the van,
Then it disappeared towards the rear of Matalan.

'CK to patrols on the Bravo, a report of Thieves On',
Tuxedo wearing sex offenders, called Hunter and Anderson,
A commended team effort, as they are both locked away,
14 years for rapes, proved by the new DNA.

A trip to the shop, to buy a grandson's birthday card,
An old lady crosses unseen, a lorry moves forward,
First to arrive, I do everything I can,
Poor Alice, 92, is trapped under a van.

On Victoria Avenue I picked your ring off the floor,
Your hand had disappeared, your fingers were no more,
An ambulance to Crumpsall, amputations, surgery,
You survived the trauma, but there's no recovery.

It's true to say... that we are stalked by Death,
So many people who I met, as they took their last breath,
Neville, Gill, Derek and Tony, to name but a few,
William at post-mortem, I looked after you.

A message to deliver, when your whole world is fine,
My cruel task will see, your life change for all time,
The message I pass, details the death of a loved one,
I walk away, your life in pieces, leaving you to mourn.

The stolen car on false plates, parked, outside his home,
Was intended for a robbery, though I couldn't have known,
As I check it I'm attacked, and a dog is set to,
I'm mauled, bleeding and unconscious, October 92.

I returned to work, with my wounds still dressed,
As a detective at Collyhurst, I tried my best,
A sweetener no doubt, but the timing was wrong,
Stressed and depressed, my recovery was long.

The effect took its toll, a significant cost,
Ambitions derailed, I felt abandoned and lost,
I knew I needed help, but I just couldn't ask,
I suppressed the feelings, and at work 'wore a mask'.

My Jury fails, they can't make a decision,
The crushing depression destroyed my ambition,
My notorious attacker, no justice to face,
Your time will come, I am on your case.

A unit is formed with covert intent,
Jim Dolan's the lead, Detective Sergeant,
Ian Eddlestone guides us as we develop our ways,
Career paths are formed from those mid 90s days.

Numerous trips to Fiddes, to get Operation names,
Hoping for a good one, that portrayed your agenda,
These were the days, long gone it would seem,
When the FIB, was just Dot and Brenda.

June 15th, 1996, a sunny Saturday,
Manchester is attacked by the IRA,
A one and a half tonne van bomb detonated,
We are in the centre of 'Town' as it's devastated.

Operations to catch robbers and drug dealers, commended,
Multiple Crown Court trials, most undefended,
Obs' Points so cold, froze my drink and food,
Stuck inside a derelict tower block
as the locks are superglued.

"Hey, O'Shea...
Do you think you could catch me if I ran away?"
Op. Fernando's 'Phoenix', soon charged with No Bail,
Remanded, convicted and locked up in Jail.

100 kilos, hidden in a secret space,
Found by 'the novice' as the 'experts' save face,
Operations in Ancoats, Collyhurst, and Cheetham Hill,
Class A drug dealers jailed, it's a real thrill.

The Drug Squad, Bradford Park, and an order from on high,
To catch a gangster whose actions saw a young child die,
After two years work, the gang's charged and remanded,
As they awaited their trial, the gangster is executed.

On a job down south, with a target in France,
A problem to solve, I take a chance,
My proposal is rejected on this occasion,
As it seems it would amount, to a military invasion!

October 99 and I am 'acting' at Bury,
A lady is lifeless, at a hotel in 'Rammy',
Strangled in her room, I give my first order,
'Tony Brown, arrest that man for murder.'

Promoted to E Relief at Stalybridge,
A Remembrance Day wreath, a true privilege,
One of my proudest moments, now and then,
*'In the morning, and at the going down of the sun,
we will remember Them'.* *

Custody Sergeant at Ashton, on New Years' Eve,
The town centre 'kicks off', 35 prisoners received,
On New Year's morning, a nervous twitch in my eye,
A lonely 7am beer, humming Auld Lang Syne.

It's all Smoke and Mirrors, to the shadows I return,
Wheels within wheels, getting 'things' done,
'Dark Arts' employed, seen but not noticed,
Our significant achievements always go unacknowledged.

To the Covert Authorities Bureau, the RIPA Unit,
Sneaky tactics for justification and to ensure an audit,
Murderers, robbers, dealers and rapists arrested,
Acknowledged by the OSC, my systems recommended.

An unexpected call from another place,
As an item of interest comes to the surface,
Too hot to handle, but I know 'a man' who will,
The recovery was my biggest thrill.

Delivering Covert training to the next generation,
Setting standards for surveillance and infiltration,
An excellent team, delivering commended courses,
Leading the way, we trained 15 Forces.

I am 6198, so I guess it was fate,
That my daughter's collar number is 16298,
I am really SO proud, but take care of her, do,
Because as well as being proud, I am terrified too.

An Inspector post, it is humbling to hear,
People I respect, call me Mr, or Sir,
I am indebted to Ric, his loyalty and commitment,
Provided me an opportunity and a final achievement.

Towards the end of my service, I become aware of a trial,
A foe from the past, a really nasty paedophile,
My work in 'the shadows', since my Jury failed,
A significant sentence, as you are finally jailed.

The demand we've faced, 200 years of evolution,
Serving and protecting, a proud institution,
Such arrogance, that politicians, for their career aspiration,
Interfere and preside over such wilful destruction.

In such a short time, 'the knowledge' disappears,
How to police, forgotten in a few short years,
We no longer 'patrol', or hunt as a pack,
Irreparable damage, it may never come back.

Government reforms have caused so much harm,
Trendy priorities, make no difference to crime,
The criminals don't care for targets and graphs,
Politicians intent on thinning the blue line.

As a service, we're broken, a sad state of affairs,
Criticised and bewildered, and nobody cares.
So I guess you have won,
you've got the police you deserve,
Dedicated but often, too busy to serve.

Five Chief Constables, Sir James Anderton was the first,
A leader of men, who's status was deserved.
David Wilmott followed, he retired a Knight,
Michael Todd died in 2008.

Then Sir Peter Fahy, who I spoke with most often,
Discussing authorities, we secured a conviction,
For the murder of a man, who's buried in the ground,
The evidence secured, but he's never been found.

Ian Hopkins was fifth, the Force needed rebuilding,
Resources stretched, the troops were struggling,
An horrific attack at the Manchester Arena,
22 lives taken, by a suicide bomber.

'I've seen things you people wouldn't believe',
Those desperate from addiction, forced to thieve,
Selling their bodies, to satisfy another's greed,
A parasitic cancer, on which misery feeds.

A career... of exposure to the worst of humanity,
Develops over time, increased negativity...,
For our fellow man..., an unhealthy suspicion,
A distrust... of people, a sad disposition.

And I've seen bravery too, and dedication,
Normal people who rightly should attract admiration,
For their thankless efforts, but there's just criticism,
From the Daily Mail and trash journalism.

I've been a part of great teams, since my first day at Bruche,
Blessed to work alongside colleagues, dedicated to truth,
B Relief, E Block, Covert teams, VC2,
The Training guys at Sedgley,
IOPS training team too.

There are so many people,
with whom I'm really proud to have served,
First class officers, of whom recognition is deserved,
To include them all in this tale, is an impossibility,
If I missed you out, I'm sorry, please accept my apology.

Special mentions to the friends who helped me along the way,
Stella, Gail, Alan, Jim, Pete, Jez and Andy,
Keith, Angie, Carmen, Vinny, Neil, Steve and Swanny,
Terry Kennedy (RIP), Melanie, Ray and Debbie.

Thorpy, Wendy, Archie, Wilkie, Darren, Lee and Tex,
Scott, Mike, Chris and Bash. Fitzy and Alex,
Trevor, Ian, Myles, Tina, Dave and Ken Blundell,
Hughie, Harry, Stuart, Derek, Mum, Dad and Michelle (X)

Eileen, Sharon, Natalie, Colin, Shelli, Denise and Bill,
Ric, Ged, Julie, Liam, Chris, Martin and Phil,
Nick, Tracey, Sean, Lindsey, Ben and Tony (x7),
Mark, Dom, Jon and those waiting in Heaven...

Because some didn't make it, their losses caused shocks,
Maggie Herron, Trigger..., Bob...,
Mark Kelly and Brian Horrocks,
And others fell..., as they served our city,
Murdered by criminals as they performed their duty.

Ray Codling,
Raj Ahmed,
Alison Armitage.
Stephen Oake,
Fiona Bone,
Nicola Hughes,
such courage.

Andy Summerscales retired,
we all know how hard he tried,
May you all rest in peace,
you served Manchester with pride.

In tears as I write this, my emotions are raw,
Memories, good and bad, and some real horror,
We all took the oath, and we stood strong and proud,
I am honoured to have served with such a special crowd.

And I'm proud to have served
in Greater Manchester Police,
The ever thinner blue line, a dedicated service,
Working hard for Manchester, the criminals we fight,
But I stand down today,
"Show me state 11. Good night."

31ˢᵗ July 2019

Rachel   (Thank you)

Excited,
Dedicated,
Buzzin',
Motivated,
Developing,
Dynamic,
Progressing,

And then...
One minute
Overwhelmed
Battered
Dominated
Hurt
Injured
Unconscious
Helpless
Humiliated
Ashamed
Embarrassed
Incapable
Foolish
Failed
Unvalued
Inferior

Ignored
Abandoned
Alone
Unworthy
Depressed
Medicated
Obsessed
Dependent
Angry
Three decades
Fucking angry.

Rachel...
Speaking,
Openly
Properly
Supported
Enabled
Encouraged
Finally
Offloading
Freely
Uninhibited
Escaping.

Rachel...
Listening,
Intently
Interested
Listening,
Recognising
Analysing
Listening,
Linking
Understanding
Interpreting
Advising
Relating
Unravelling
Converting
Releasing
Recovering
27 years.

Service

The prisoners revolted
An inmate assaulted
I was with you when you died.

A device detonated
A city centre devastated
I was there as glass fell from the sky,

An old lady is stuck
Underneath a truck
Her cries still haunt my mind.

When you wanted to drown
I fought you down
Your 'Stay Alive' note was kind.

A gangster executed
His body, I located
The hands, silently... screamed.

When you ended your days
K3-09 in Strangeways
Your felony was redeemed.

A prison suicide
Hung at dawn
A noose from torn up prison sheets.

The heroin dealers
Exploiting the weak
We took them off the streets.

As you took your last breath
I reported your death
Ensuring that the evidence was true.

As they opened your chest
For a Coronial inquest
I was there looking inside you.

At the Coroner's Court
I delivered my report
About an acquaintance I'd never met.

An arsenal recovered
The evidence secured
We neutralised the threat.

People kidnapped and tortured
As a gang war, erupted
The things you did were just evil.

The whole gang captured
For years incarcerated
The repercussions, still so real.

When they kicked in your door
And raped you on the floor
We caught them and put them away.

We chased their car
They didn't run far
Their crimes proved by DNA.

Whilst doing my job
I was attacked by a yob
Bleeding, unconscious, defeated.

Memories,
Of moments, of times now passed,
That so many take for granted.

And when I moved on
Some people 'welcomed me' me with scorn
The scowls on their faces betrayed...

The contempt that they feel
For the job that I did
For 30 years, 3 months and 15 days.

Moving On

When I sit and recount
The things I have seen
The steps I have walked
The places I've been
The people I met
Good times and bad
The experiences
Happy and sad

The things people did
The things that we stopped
The chaos we faced
The people we copped
And those we didn't
The ones that got away
Solaced by the knowledge
'They'll come another day'

And now I'm retired
A different me exists
How quickly I've detached
But the bad guys persist
The crime, the greed
A place where no one cares
The abuse and exploitation
But I'm now blissfully unaware.

ACAB

All coppers are bastards
but who dragged you clear?
of the car you'd been racing
whilst bladdered on beer

All coppers are bastards
and other vile names
but who risked their life?
as it burst into flames

All coppers are bastards
but who rushed to your aid?
when by anonymous phone call
death threats were made

All coppers are bastards
but who saved your life?
when you were stabbed in the leg
with a kitchen knife

All coppers are bastards
but who did you hound?
when the 'big boys' you 'play with'
were on their way around

All coppers are bastards
but we weren't your foes
when a rival drug dealer
shot out your windows

All coppers are bastards
but when it all came on top
it was us that you turned to
you needed a cop

All coppers are bastards
until your past caught up
When the Karma you'd earned
got you all smashed up

All coppers are bastards
But who stopped the bleeding?
when you got yourself shot
For our help you were pleading

Some coppers didn't book off
At the end of their shift
An eternal duty
Their families bereft.

www.ukpolicememorial.com

Covid 19

For Marcia and Margaret
May you both rest in peace

PAN(dem)IC

No milk, loo rolls or pasta
At Morrison's, Tesco or Asda
No hand wash or tinned tomatoes
At Aldi, Lidl or Waitrose
No eggs at the corner shop
or meat at the local Co Op
At the Spar, there's no paracetamol
No beans or chicken or mince
And when it comes to washing your hands
You've got to sanitise, not rinse

But there's no sanitiser or hand wash
And there's no football on the telly
The Euros are postponed until next year
And I'm starting to fancy a bevvy
But when it comes to the pub, we're all barred
Boris has grounded the Nation
This is starting to get quite hard
I think that we might need to ration

Because there's no common sense in this crisis
Whilst I'm at work you've emptied the shelves
I just want to get food for my family
But you've taken care of yourselves
No one at Asda stops you buying
So much more than you actually need
Five loaves and eight packs of chicken
How many do you have to feed?

It's getting like The Walking Dead
And we're closing all the schools
People are buying extra fridge freezers
These are the real fools
Storing food, they bought but don't need
Without regard for anybody
Lives obsessed with greed
With no regrets for any bodies

I drove 35 miles, for a pint of milk
So Mum and Dad can have a cup of tea
But I'm not allowed to visit them
It's video calls for me
Their ages and existing conditions
Mean they're locked down for 20 weeks
I check in on them daily
And place virtual kisses on their cheeks

The Summer holiday's cancelled
The cinemas and restaurants are deserted
So many stores are closing
And the staff are all getting flirted

So I'm going for a long walk
I'll maybe feed the Swans
Two beautiful birds, totally unaware
Of the selfishness that's going on.

Stay at Home (for Marcia)

I'm becoming increasingly concerned
About the Coronavirus
It seems, as more is learned
Covid19 wants to kill us

We had Boris at the helm
The shock as he became ill
Our Nation becoming overwhelmed
This Virus is here to kill

A friend and colleague has already died
'Marcia' was her name
She fought, she fought, she really tried
But it took her all the same

This Virus is here, right here, right now
And needs a host, to stay alive
You need to stop it moving around
If your family is to survive

So stay in, stay at home, don't go out
For the sake of your partner
your husbands, your wives

Your parents, your kids
Your family and friends
Staying in could save their lives.

Marcia Pryce 16th June 1958 - 2nd April 2020

Wet Markets

Damp
Moist
dirty.
Fluids
deposits
from questionable practices
and questionable standards
consequential spillages
carelessness
neglect
in every sense.
Irresponsible
ignorant
with consequence
and consequences,
wet.

The Best and the Worst

In difficult times
A particular type
Of person rises to the surface
Comes to the fore
Takes to the floor
Responsibility and service.

The NHS, Doctors and Nurses
The cleaners and backroom support

Police officers, Regulars and Specials
Step forward to hold the Fort

Civil Servants
Coordinate
To ensure that things are in place

Factory workers
Produce the things
That we need, from day to day

Truck Drivers
Logistics, Moving goods
So we have the things we need

Supermarket staff
Stocking shelves
or on tills
To make sure that we can feed

The Bin Men
Who move our rubbish
Prevent infestation by pests

The volunteers
Who fill any gaps
Omitted by the rest

And the public
With their Thursday Claps
Sitting out this lockdown time.

But...

In such times
Increasingly so... (it would seem,)
Are those with different agendas
People who hold none of the values
Of those who step up to defend us

The locusts, who selfishly
Created panic, buying, everything
Those ignoring, clear instructions
That would stop the virus spreading

The Fake Newsers, And their online lies
Intensifying the fear
The haters, typing internet vile
About Boris in intensive care

Anonymous keyboard warriors
Who type, but contribute nothing

The best and worst
Of our Society
The disparity is stunning.

Socially Distanced

I'd love to hug you
And pick you up
And squeeze you
And give you a kiss

But we're kept apart
Socially Distanced
Strange times
I've known nothing like this

I get your shopping
(Or what I can), and leave it at your door

The roads are empty, as I drive home
And stay indoors, once more

Petrol is cheaper, not that I need any
I've not filled up for over three months

Pollution, reducing
I think the air is cleaner
Or maybe it's just a hunch

We video chat
About this and that
Technology like an IT Hub

But when this is over
I'll kiss you and hug you
And we can have tea at the Pub.

Happy Birthday Mum

I'm finding today quite difficult
It's not the way we say
'Many Happy Returns'
On a family birthday
With everyone apart
When we should all be together
What a day we could have had
With such lovely weather
So although you're both locked down
I wrote this rhyme to say
We'll get together once this has passed
To celebrate your day.

Rainbow Ribbons

Rainbow ribbons
Adorn the doors
Of houses around our town
A message of 'Thanks'
To those Key Workers
Who worked throughout Lockdown.

The NHS
Police and Fire
Teachers and Councils too
Lorry Drivers
And Supermarket staff
You all helped get us through.

As Lockdown eases
A 'normality' returns
A foot returns to the pedal
Recognition
Is rightly due
You all deserve a Medal.

Only When it Rains

I noticed that you weren't out today
That was odd, I supposed
Coz you have all been out every day
Since lockdown was imposed.

But I guess there's no need to worry
About why you chose to abstain
It isn't because you are ill at all
It's coz it is pouring down with rain.

So despite the deadly pandemic
If it's sunny, you're always outside
But only when it's pouring with rain
Do you actually stay inside.

If you stop to think how crazy that is
You'll see that there really is no doubt
That taking such risks is killing people
So stay in, stay at home, don't go out.

I'm Sick

I'm sick of people
Leaving litter on beaches
I'm sick of Coronavirus speeches

I'm sick of the queues
At the supermarket
I'm sick of the Government's
Track and Trace widget

I'm sick of cheap petrol
When I've nowhere to go
I'm sick of 'Two Metres'
And my mood being low

I'm sick of the ignorant
And I'm sick of 'The R'
I'm sick of shut pubs
I want to visit a Bar

I'm sick of stupid people
Where danger exists
I'm sick of people dying
From a virus that persists

I'm sick of washing my hands
I'm sick of hand sanitiser
I'm sick of wearing a mask
I'm sick of "being in it together"

I'm sick of media agendas
And those who believe them
Why doesn't anyone speak out?
Why do people accept them?

I'm sick of the media
I'm sick of the BBC
I'm sick of representatives
That don't represent me

I'm sick of the lies
I'm sick of the fiction
Professed by the media
To provoke a reaction

I'm sick of politicians
Politicians on all sides
I'm sick of the divisions
And those who divide

I'm sick of Boris Johnson
And antiseptic wipes
I'm sick of Kier Starmer
And his opportunistic snipes

I'm sick of Dom Cummings
I'm sick of MPs
Who dictate to the nation
But then do as they please

I'm sick of correspondents
Spouting opinions on the news
And their pretentious bookshelves
Displayed on interviews

I'm sick of the news
And the Daily Update
I'm sick of the tension
I'm sick of the hate

I'm sick about US Cops
Killing again
I'm sick that UK Cops
Keep getting blamed

I'm sick of statues
of enslavers in Town
I'm sick of the mob
that tears them down

I'm sick of conflict
For conflict's sake
I'm sick of social media
And news that is fake

I'm sick of being a white
heterosexual male
And being held responsible
For every Societal fail

I'm sick of being accused
I'm sick of being racist
I'm sick of being guilty
On a historical basis

I'm sick of the anarchists
I'm sick of the fascists
I'm sick of looting
Being considered a protest

I'm sick of protesters
With their placards and banners
I'm sick of people
Without standards or manners

I'm sick of war memorials
being defaced
I'm sick of our nation
being disgraced

I'm sick of seeing UK Cops
Bending their knee
And facing a Mob
Without PPE

I'm sick of isolation
From friends and family
I'm sick of social distancing
I long for normality.

Strange Times

We looked to Boris
For what to do
Most stayed at home
As they were told to
Scared of each other in the Supermarket queue
No doubt, this is a very strange time.

Mother's Day cancelled
She's in Quarantine
Exams cancelled, what will the Grades mean?
Will this strange situation
Become our new routine?
The strangest, strangest of times.

Football cancelled
Video calling
Holidays cancelled
Hand sanitising
Birthdays cancelled
Clearly defining
That these, are the strangest of times.

The roads are quiet
And there's cleaner air
But the barber's is shut, have you *seen* my hair?
We're socially distanced
No hugs to share
In these strangest of times.

At Morrison's and Asda
(The only places I go)
Keeping a gap of 2 metres
As I follow the arrow
Almost impossible
The aisle is so narrow
Strange, strange times.

The 'R' below 1
Now a National obsession
"Hello, are you OK?"
Is now a literal question
A mask that now covers
Your facial expression
In these very strange times.

So many killed
But there's nothing to see
The funeral of a friend
How can it be...
That I can't attend
With her family?

...

Strange times.

The Media

I've stopped listening to the radio
I've stopped watching the news
My depression is at overflow
They're giving me the blues

So I'm listening to birdsong
As they're flying overhead
They lift my soul, from this news sinkhole
And the lies they'd have us fed.

Our Prison

"There is No Planet B"

Our Prison

The superior being, the most complex mind
A two-legged animal, known as Mankind
Limitless potential, achievement and creation
Earth dominated and Space Exploration.

There's another truth, it could be said
Needless, deliberate, suffering inflicted
Killing for fun, to feel superior
Only serves to prove, Mankind is inferior.

Unimaginable cruelty... Imagined and brought
Unthinkable brutality... brutally thought
Developed, created and sold by a man
Enabling psychopaths to kill whatever they can.

Machines constructed by creative minds
To kill people and animals of every kind
Regardless, for profit, though no threat was present
Your brilliance wasted, as is your talent.

It must take a certain type, of unkind...
Dysfunctional individual with a not right mind
To pay money to secure, a kick or a thrill
Effectively buying, the right to kill.

The focus of your destruction, has a common theme
Often the biggest, or fastest or rarest being
Hippos, Crocodiles and Alligators
Any kind of deer, to take its antlers.

A Caspian Tiger, a Barbary Lion
Species we can no longer cast an eye on
Forever, due to selfish immorality
You shot a giraffe as it ate leaves from a tree.

Rhino, Leopards, Bears and Wolves
Anything is 'Game', if it lives and moves
A sniper shot to take a zebra
It's just a horse in a striped pyjama.

As a young child, did you long...
To torture and kill? When did you go wrong?
What happened to make you turn
Into a killer who likes killing for fun?

It doesn't do justice, to describe you as immoral
Selfish, destructive, psychopathic and brutal
From your position, you might think that a bit hard
From my position, you're an inadequate bastard.

The need to be recognised as the last one to kill
An African Elephant, or a Jaguar in Brazil
Your ultimate kick, to achieve the distinction
That it was you, who secured a species extinction.

I don't understand your sick disposition
Killing an animal, for your trophy collection
And when there's nothing left, what will you do then?
Perhaps, buy a licence, to allow you to kill men.

A prolific parasite, indiscriminate destruction
Desensitised by defect, devoid of compassion
With brutal efficiency, you cause animals to suffer
Nature will intervene, to allow the world to recover.

Man's Best Friend

A relationship repeated a million times over
One man and his dog
His Master's Voice
Sheep Dog
Police Dog
Guide dogs for the blind
More than a pet, loyalty defined.

Your every move monitored, with anticipation
That the reason you got up
Might bring some attention
A stroke
A snack
Or maybe small talk
Or if I'm really lucky, we'll go for a walk.

A knock at the door, a chance to pretend
That I am ready and strong
And able to defend
The postman
The Paperboy
The window cleaner
All threats, to my mind, I'll see off the offender.

A ball or a rope, anything you want to do
I'm happy to do anything
If I'm with you
Stay in, Go out
Do nothing, that's fine
We'll stay here at home, we can both have a whine.

Then... I am taken... by a less loving man
Who came by one day
And put me in a van
Other dogs
No food
And nothing to do
No sign of my owner, does he miss me too?

I'm stuck in a cage, next to another hound
There's a treadmill
And a tyre to drag around
No love
No play
It's all very stressed
Some dogs disappear, some come back a mess.

I'm taken to a building, there are lots of men
Some other dogs
But I don't know them
Thrown in
Shouting
I'm bitten and injured
I have to fight back, I'm bleeding and cornered.

The cheers and jeers of the men that surround
The pit we are in
It's a frightening sound
Fighting
Biting
I'm under attack
Unsure what to do, I need to fight back

Suddenly, I know, I've been got by the throat
The other dog has me
I'm in trouble, I know
Breathing...
Bleeding...
The pain seems unreal
Shouting, noises... quieting, it's strange how I feel.

I was no match, the other dog won
I'm lying, dying
The men had their fun
Injured
Killed
No need for a vet
For the price of my life, some men won a bet.

The Fox

A dependant industry centred around
Terriers, horses and hunting with hounds
Maintained and raised for just one purpose
To perpetuate cruelty and a culture so pompous.

A timid red dog is the subject of their attention
She lives in a Den, sub rural accommodation
The Red Fox, a mostly nocturnal creature
Widespread in our land, an indigenous feature.

Your farmland was their home, their natural domain
Ownership assumed, to farm cattle or grain
The fox strays into a barn, by hunger she's driven
For such a trespass, she will not be forgiven.

There's a social side to the hunt that alludes
To counter the truth for the killing they do
Charity dinners, social propaganda, community events
With a hierarchical structure to ensure obedience.

There's those who 'belong', with their stories and fables
Members of the Hunt, who own horses and stables
This psychopathic community, Lorded as Gentry
Conspirators to this cruel and pretentious barbarity.

Others follow the hunt, some watch from afar
They eat their sycophant picnic whilst sat in their car
'Hangers on', who long for social ascension
Their inadequate lives, desperate for inclusion.

'A country pursuit', this is humanity corrupted
So diabolically cruel and totally outdated
'A way of life', this is morally bankrupted
So much so, it was legislated.

But the hunts continue, the lies they tell
"It was just a Drag Hunt but the hounds picked up the smell
Of a fox who had recently passed through the trail
We tried to recover the hounds, but unfortunately failed."

The Hounds, unfed, to ensure they are eager
Run out of control to the danger of road users
The pack in a garden, recklessly mistaken
Domestic pets, collaterally taken.

The hounds have a scent, the Huntsmen direct the pack
The 'whippers in' keep the hounds on track
The blood raising sound of the Huntsman's horn
"Tally Ho!" he calls, as the Hunt is urged on.

The chase has commenced, but the Den's entrance is locked
The Earth Stoppers made sure that the foxhole is blocked
To stop this night-time forager getting home any way
To ensure this nocturnal dog can be hunted by day.

She is exposed and unable to take sanctuary
Vulnerable to your premeditated cruelty
She will run for her life and if caught, she will die
Torn apart and disembowelled, a blood lust satisfied.

Blooding of new initiates, surely child abuse?
Encouraged by adults, how could they refuse?
The master of the hunt, a 'title' so grand
The corruption of children, before they understand.

A hypocritical hierarchy, for the amusement of men
A small dog torn apart with cubs left in the Den
The Terrier men, will come back for her Cubs
They'll be reared by the hunt to 'train' the pups.

Reviled as a pest, but bred to ensure
A socially accepted cruelty endures
The cubs that remain are raised to make sure
That despite the killing, there's plenty in store.

The Hare

Another victim, of a cruel and idle mind
A harmless creature, persecuted by mankind
Energy spent, escaping competing lurchers
Themselves, exploited, by men and their wagers.

The Waterloo Cup, now banned by enactment
Continues unofficially on fields nationwide
The quarry has no choice, a victim of entrapment
The fields are open, and there's nowhere to hide.

Over a short distance, the hare is faster
Canine stamina over Leporidae terror
Next time will be harder, if he survives this round
as if a rope in a tug of war between two hounds.

Then, caught...

This is what it is to be 'quickly dispatched'
An end I'm sure we'd all choose to avoid
If given the option to be torn apart
Proof of man's compassionate void.

The Badger

A shy, but nonetheless capable creature
Almost only a nocturnal feature
Of gardens and pastures, as it forages for food
To feed the mouths in its underground brood.

Distinctive colours, an unmistakable suit
A black and white mask, and a grey overcoat
This elusive soul suffered such persecution
That it became the subject of its own legislation.

Despite legal intent, they get little protection
The source of TB, the farmers allegation
DEFRA licenses permit indiscriminate culling
Whatever you call it, it's really just killing.

What type of person, goes to work each day?
To a job where they are tasked to kill caged animals.
And what is the impact upon their minds?
Or has desensitisation happened in their past times?

Despite years of 'research', The allegation is unproved
Bovine TB still infects the cloven hooved
An expensive and ineffective approach to the problem
Tens of thousands of deaths but TB hasn't gone.

And then, there's the Baiters...

The men with a spade
Who arrive at the Sett intent to invade
Bringing dogs and clubs, the escape routes are blocked
As the digging begins, gas capsules are dropped.

And the dogs are 'Set To', to amuse the men
Their psychopathic amusement, and worthless bets
The terriers sent down tunnels, to flush out their quarry
Injuries suffered that won't be treated by Vets.

An unwinnable fight, because the stronger he is
The men with dogs, more they release
As he weakens through injury, overwhelmed
He questions why they came to his realm.

And the dogs suffer too, the Badgers are strong
They'll fight to defend their home and their young
But it's the men, not the dogs who are the true enemies
They avoid any threat, suffer no injuries.

Then when it's over, the Badger lies dead
The Sett is destroyed, the grey overcoat, red
I can't comprehend, enjoyment from cruelty
These human monsters exist in our community.

The Stag

A magnificent stag, with a 16-point crown
That he has earned the right to wear
The pride of the herd, dominant on the downs
No other can compare.

His Points and Blades are not yours to steal
You have no right to acquire
His antlers are not a trophy
For you to mount on your wall and admire.

A dozen miles, then he hides in the trees
Exhausted, his energy spent
But then seen and cornered
A single shot, concludes this 'sporting' event.

How can such an act be performed with pride?
Those involved should never own a gun
How can such evil, be considered sport?
Violent psychopaths who kill for fun.

The Bull

The Running of the Bulls and 'La Corrida de Toros'
An event devoid of culture or kudos
He really hasn't got a chance
Capabilities negated in advance.

He is taunted for your cruel satisfaction
Panicked hooves on cobbles, that provide no traction
His horns are blunted, to remove his threat
To add to his torment, fireworks are set.

The first encounter, he doesn't understand
But the men have done this, many times before
What are they doing? What are the rules?
Developed expertise, deployed to confuse.

Weaknesses magnified, escape routes blocked
Tactics to ensure his suffering is mocked
Pierced, humiliated and tormented to ensure
He's weakened before he meets 'El Matador'.

A single bull, against all these cowards
Each pushing their victim to the point of frenzy
Encircled, provoked, tormented and stabbed
A premeditated act of Mediterranean cruelty.

The inevitable stumbles, as he charges through the streets
A festival of evil, devoid of humanity
Distractions provide routes for his tormentors to flee
Ignorant of the humility of this amazing beast.

His attempts to escape, confirm the futility
A shameful spectacle of human brutality
Processes developed to frustrate and torture
A designed advantage for the 'brave' Matador.

Starved and thirsty, drugged and beaten
En la Plaza de Toros, for the final Act
Spirit tormented, mentally broken
A sword at hand, ready to despatch.

A once proud beast, now destroyed and abused
The appreciative audience, sickeningly amused
As eventually he falls, ending his ordeal
The roses rain down, in psychopathic approval.

The Rhinoceros

A peaceful beast, who's only need
Is to graze the savannas, with young to feed
The rhinoceros, a 2-tonne herbivore
Is destined... to exist, no more

In family groups, presents no threat
This gentle beast, with a facial bayonet
A massive creature whose looks impose
Cursed by a Keratin horn on its nose

Ignorant men, devoid of mercy
Prize the horns, desperate for money
To sell into Oriental medicine
This evil trade is so obscene

An armoured hide, designed by nature
To protect this amazing creature
From predators, in its natural ground
Won't protect against a rifle round

Keratin: fingernails, hair and hooves
They even break into museums and zoos
To steal the horns, their mistaken belief
That it's medicinal properties, might provide relief

So now the rhino is endangered
Global numbers depleted
Nola, a Northern White rhinoceros
The last example of a doomed species.

The Elephant

The largest land mammal, *Loxodonta*
A 6-tonne soul with no natural predator
A 70-year life expectancy
A nomadic life of family dependency.

Habitual visitors following ancestral paths
Visiting water holes, year after year
One report, you walked through the house of a man
Who'd built his abode, on a route of your clan.

A familial herd of beauty and grace
Huge, clumsy and easy to trace
Some roam sub Saharan Africa
Others native to India, Nepal and Sri Lanka.

Cursed by the tusks that adorn your face
The Ivory adornment, that distinguish your 'race'
A family unit, several generations
Caring for each other, through constant migrations.

Nurturing young as the plains you cross
Celebrating birth, mourning loss
Nursery behaviour, extended family
Matriarchal herds of maternity.

Grief, joy, play and anger, as your journey continues
The unjustifiable evil on your route, pursues
A mother falls, the herd is bereft
All ivory is murder, desecration and theft.

The Vultures

An ugly bird, perfectly designed
To perform a function, to break open the hide
Of a creature, fallen in the wild, now dead
Nature recycles, everything gets fed.

Their instinctive behaviour, circling overhead
Betrays the position, where the creature lies dead
An unintended consequence, that often indicates
The precise location where a Poacher operates.

It's their circling above, that attracts the attention
Of a Ranger committed, to animal protection
This signal suggests, a crime may have occurred
A poaching attack launched on the herd.

The Rangers set off to investigate and protect
The crime, if committed, they will try to detect
Ivory from an elephant, or a rhino horn
These creatures killed faster than their young can be born.

So the vulture has become an unintended threat
A simple solution, and highly effective
The poacher's response, inevitably brutal
Is to poison the carcass, and the vulture collective.

A selfish act, to indiscriminately poison
All the scavengers, who feed on carrion
Lions, hyenas and vultures are killed
To make sure the poachers work is not signalled.

So when an animal falls through natural causes
There are no longer the necessary vultures
To open the carcass, so all can eat
Instead, the body lies there in the heat.

And before too long, the carcass is unfit
Whilst others who would naturally benefit
Go without, unable to feed
They slowly starve, because of Man's greed.

The Whale

The biggest creature, ever, on Earth
Up to 200 tonnes, and submerged from birth
Sharing the family name, Cataceans
Constantly moving through seas and oceans

Complex, cooperative social pods
Familial units, intelligent 'bods'
A compassionate creature, risk aware
Known to protect humans, when a shark is near

The need to breathe, brings them to the surface
To be greeted by a Japanese face
Exploiting this natural dependency
The blood that is spilt will create a red sea

The Faroe Islands and their questionable culture
Pilot Whales, another 'school' massacre
The pod is herded and trapped, then slaughtered
A cruelly efficient and barbaric method

Strandings caused by shipping sonar
Resulting in a pod stranded and beached
Ignorance contributes to this recurring horror
A duty of care neglectfully breached.

Natural Causes

Strengths and weaknesses, developed by evolution
Nature provided food, water and climate
Balances maintained by natural regulation
Greed and ignorance now threaten to destroy it

Everything is a superior but to something inferior
Everything has its place, a purpose in nature's scheme
Abilities and vulnerabilities, like Rock, Paper, Scissors
A natural Utopia, Nature's aspirational dream

There's a natural consequence for every occurrence
A reaction for every action, or inaction
Our activities risk an unnatural imbalance
This the cost of human progression

Natural law doesn't allow for negotiation
Mankind cannot tame the extremes of our weather
There is no scope for interpretation
When something is 'gone', then it's gone forever

Unintelligent interference by an intelligent bald ape
To maximise profit from natural sources
Using unnatural means to maximise the exploit...
Pillaging the world and destroying resources

Such disregard for the animals, that share the Earth
To allow a man to own and farm a field
What right have we, to destroy their place of birth?
To raise a herd of cows for the beef they will yield

Survival of the fittest doesn't really apply
If species disappear at an unprecedented rate
everything's getting ill, and likely to die
So many different threats to each creature's fate

Habitat stolen and devastated
At unsustainable rates, that will soon ensure
Natural occupants killed or evicted
Habitats and species are lost for evermore

Animals destroyed for a horn, tusk or pelt
There's a reason why the water is not fit to drink
Temperatures increase, the Polar ice caps melt
After decades of ignorance, the oceans stink

The sea is a rubbish tip, uninhabitable habitat
The home of the whales, the seas, the ocean
Polluted, a poisonous putrid vat
The origin of life is now a toxic prison

Articles and particles, abnormal PH balances
Acid rain, buildings dissolve, unattributable consequences
So if nobody is individually, held responsible or blamed
We'll carry on regardless, until our environment is flamed

There's a delicate balance, between hostile and habitable
Everything has its proper place, purpose and function
Bacteria, to bug, to bird, to reptile, to mammal
But if one link breaks, the whole environment will weaken

Nature deals and recovers from natural events
Volcanos and hurricanes, natural creativity unimpaired
Extremes of heat or cold, are natural compliments
But we assault the world faster than our damage can be
repaired

But another risk looms, what if She fought back?
As the waters rise, now our habitat is threatened
has She already commenced her attack?
There are consequences,
and on this Earth, we're imprisoned

The air we breathe contains so many ills
The food we eat, is mechanically recovered
The water we drink, contains hormones from pills
Now all conspire, to avenge Nature's Mother

We've thrived and evolved to a point of domination
What next for Nature's 8 billion, ignorant guests?
An unintended position with a natural solution
A species of all consuming, out of control pests.

Hollins Vale

A Nature Reserve,
and a refuge for stressed minds.

A Walk in Hollins Vale Nature Reserve

Once over the 66, I'm in a different world
As natural glory begins to unfurl
My feet on the cobbles, as I walk down the lane
A soulful connection awakens again

The pace of life slows
The air in my nose
The noise disappears
The sounds in my ears
The things, that are now heard
Like a nearby bird
An escape from the madness
And a cure for my sadness

A fearless Robin makes a pledge
A tiny Wren sings in the hedge
A Grey Wagtail's, tail-wagging display
Whilst a flock... of Long Tailed Tits play

A Woodpecker, tap tap tapping
A Wood Pigeon's... panicked flapping
A Common Tern hovers above the lake
A Jay and the dreadful sounds they make

The Chiffchaff, alarms
A Goldfinch, charms
The delicate butterflies
Delicately, flutter by

A Tawney Owl's hoot
The Swans... They are Mute
A Moorhen's red beak
The white beak is a Coot

So distinctive... Peewits or Lapwings?
A tiny Goldcrest, in a fern tree, sings
A Blue Tit, a Great Tit
House Martins and Swallows
Dunnocks, Rooks and Carrion Crows
A Chaffinch, a Greenfinch, a Bullfinch too
A rare Ring Ouzel, just passing through

A territorial Blackbird, chases off rivals
A Tree Creeper, creeps up a tree in spirals
In Hollins Brook, I spotted a Dipper
Nearby, the evidence of another fly-tipper

A Roe Deer, bolts, towards the landfill
An unforgettable moment, a real thrill
A Greylag Goose, A Great Crested Grebe
At Pilsworth, I see a Bunting in the Reeds

A Kingfisher in flight, with a blue and red coat
A Song Thrush competes
with a singing White Throat
Sparrowhawks, keeping watch from a tree
The Heron, ... flying away from me

A pair of Buzzards soaring above
A pair of loved up, Collared Doves
A Cormorant, a Little Grebe, a Tufted Duck
So many Magpies, I'm due some good luck

An aggressive, male, Canada Goose
A rumour, there's a 'Big Cat' on the loose
A Kestrel, hovers, to observe
The beauty of Hollins Vale Nature Reserve.

The Swans

Throughout Coronavirus Lockdown
The Swans in Hollins Vale
Provided hope to many folk
That goodness would prevail

For seven weeks, she's dedicated
Almost every hour
Eight eggs lovingly incubated
Through both sunshine and shower

The hope that was once promised
It seems has sadly passed
These pods of love, of life and hope
Lie silent in the nest.

The Goose

The embers and ashes still radiating
Empty cans and snap bags, clearly betraying
The time that you spent here, intoxicating
From last night, to today's early hours

The scene, I find, an image of ignorance
Your idle times, attract my abhorrence
Your behaviour, self-centred, such arrogance
Your lifestyle simply devours

At some point overnight, from where you have set camp
A shotgun was discharged, by the light of a lamp
The spent cartridges lie, on the grass where I tramp
This morning, as I walk around the lake

In the water, a body that you dispatched
A Canada Goose, it's eggs, unhatched
A cruel consequence, stupidity, unmatched
How many lives do you take?

Fly Tipping

Shall I compare thee to a parasite?
A selfish lowlife, an ignorant man
Your own needs met, as you tip in the night
In a flat back truck or tatty old van
A remote location to mask the noise
Sneaking down a lane, or a public park
Mattresses, tyres, a load of old toys
Plasterboard and rubble, dumped in the dark
Garden waste, furniture, thrown from a bridge
They'll rot there forever, but you don't care
As you tip in the night, a broken fridge
Dumped in a river, a settee and chairs
A freezer; bin bags... full of dead chickens
A clear health risk, you don't give a Dickens.

The Trees

Guardians of the lane
Over decades passed
Gone forever
With the Woodpeckers nest
Because Garic cut down the trees

A Protection Order
has no effect
Bury Council
Doesn't care to protect
So Garic cut down the trees

74 bird species
That I've seen in the Vale
No Woodpeckers recently
Doesn't that tell a tale?
Since Garic cut down the trees.

A Wet Day in May

Today in Hollins Vale Nature Reserve
I got a drenching I didn't deserve
My task, to make sure that the swans got fed
Whilst more sensible folk stayed in their beds

Before I left home, I'd checked the weather online
"Fine early on, then showers after nine"
An unexpected turn, around ten past seven
A torrent of H_2O from the heavens

The hard-baked paths, have soon turned soggy
The fields around the Vale, now boggy
The footprints, 'fossilised' since they were trodden
Already softened and totally sodden

So, as rain stopped play, I tramp back to my abode
My socks are wet, my hands are cold
No photos today, there's been nowt to see
Just swans, the geese, some ducks, and me.

Hollins Brook

Today
the Brook runs in blue and gold
an oily discharge
from where untold
upwind in the Vale
an acrid smell
risk of death
to the birds who dwell
within this stream
and on the banks
nearby
where someone emptied tanks
and set their excess
oil to drain
mixed with gentle summer rain
encouraging the stream,
'Faster, faster'
dispersing our own
'Exxon Valdez' disaster
via the Roch, the Irwell, and the Mersey
sending the slick
towards the sea
what chance for the Kingfisher?
Or the wildlife I see?
What chance for your kids?
Fish fingers for tea?

Others

Miscellaneous poems

Two Minutes

Sixteen million killed, in World War One
Sixty million in 'The Second'
Often just lads, with a dream of adventure
Where Service and National Pride beckoned.

The 'misrepresentation' of their prospects
That masked what they were destined to endure
The hidden truth of what lay ahead
The unimaginable horror.

Since the 'War to end all wars'
We've had many new 'Campaigns'
Each the source of a family's grief
A young soldier's repatriated remains.

Lifetimes lived, so much time has now passed
Those of us who now reside
In this green and pleasant land
Never knew those Men who died.

So, the least that we, 'The Many' can do
Is to stop... and pause to remember
The sacrifices, of 'The Few'
On the 11th day of November.

Pals

When they were 'called'
They marched off to battle
These Pals from Lancashire.

To fight the wars
And defend the Realm
Against hostile gunfire.

A cross now stands
Bearing the names
Of so many deceased young men.

A small white Gravestone
where they now rest
They never saw their village again.

The Angels of The North

They dug for coal
They worked the Mills
They filled the canals
Beneath Lancashire hills

With coal and cotton
And steel and food
The barges filled with
Produce and goods

The canals became
Britain's arteries
Carrying the machines
They built in factories

And they farmed the fields
With picks and shovels
They lived in squalor
In dreadful hovels

No choice but to work
What cost to their health?
Enriching the nation
Generating wealth

As the nation prospered
Through their toil
Northern cotton towns
began to sprawl

Populating recruitment grounds...
For future wars
These people,
the forgotten Angels
of the North

Who died by the thousand
Worked to their graves
No reward for their labour
These Angels were slaves.

A Chance Encounter

A Lakeland hike, near Bassenthwaite
A trip to the top of Dodd Fell
We stop on route to Osprey watch
And see Red Squirrels as well.

To spot my first wild Ospreys
Gives me such a kick
These rare and awesome predators
Have raised another chick.

The walk resumes through forestry works
Then natural fauna wins through
The Peacock butterflies in flight
There are dozens on our route.

"Wait!... Just there, a bird, on the path
Can you see it? Waging its tail?
"What is it? It seems quite small
It's hard to get the scale.

"Get the camera, take some photos"
Snap, Snap, Snap, "Did you get it?"
The images confirm, the bird we saw,
My first Meadow Pipit.

Unfair, to compare, to the Ospreys
In all their glory and their might
But a chance encounter
With this little soul, gave me just as much delight.

Headaches

A cowardly thing
That attacks when I'm weakest
In the middle of a crisis, you seek me out.

Whether it's a virus, or stress
You have no conscience
When I'm least able to respond, you wipe me out.

Or are you my 'reward'?
For getting through
Once the job is done, you cut me down.

The pain that grows
In the centre of my mind
A special place reserved for you.

Now for however many days
No potions work
Your storm moves in
I am possessed by you.

In time you'll pass
Until then I am crushed
And when you have passed
I'm exhausted and bruised.

And then you're gone
I'll take time to recover
I know you'll return
When I'm confused.

Imagine, What If?

What if things weren't as they are?
Imagine life without a car?
What if you had no mobile phone?
What if you didn't have a home?
I mean, really... what if you were homeless?
Where would you put your stuff?
What if you lost your job?
Imagine living rough?
No bedroom, No bathroom, No kitchen...
No high-speed wireless connection...
or Freeview, no tele... Imagine it...
What if there was no internet?
What if you had no fridge freezer?
How would we keep our meat?
What if you had no bread?
What if you had nothing to eat?
How would you feed the birds...?

How would you hang up the washing...?
if you had no pegs
What if you didn't have a washing machine?
What if you had no legs?
Imagine needing a wheelchair...
How different your life would be,
What if you lost your hearing?
What if you couldn't see?

Imagine if you went deaf?
Imagine being blind?
What if you didn't understand... anything?
What if you lost your mind?

What if you didn't recognise yourself?
Your kids? Your family?
What if your life was desperate?
What if you had no money?

What if you lived on skid row?
What if you had no friends?
What if you had nowhere to go?
No Christmas cards to send?
What if you were lonely?
What if nobody cared?
What if you had no family?
Imagine...

The Tram

There used to be a train, from Bury Interchange
A British Rail rattler, that I'm sure had mange...
In the horsehair seats, that were decades old,
The windows wet in response to the cold

Smoking carriages and the rancid fumes...
Emanating from the waiting rooms
So in July 91, (and not before time)
The 'powers that be' finally closed the line
There were no protests, nobody cried
It wasn't sad, there were no fond goodbyes.

Some ten months passed, before we heard the 'hoot'
Of a Metrolink Tram, on its Maiden route
Between Bury Interchange and Victoria Station
The first 'modern street rail system' in the Nation

That was soon extended to Altrincham
A traffic solution to reduce the Jams
As it crossed the City, that it helped to revive
It felt like 'The Future' had finally arrived

Then a line through to Eccles, more accessibility
And a branch breaking off to Media City
Rochdale, Oldham, Ashton Under Lyne
St. Werburgh's Road on the Airport line

East Didsbury followed as did Exchange Square
It's only a minute walk from Victoria to there.
Tickets from machines for cash, then contactless
Now 'Tapping in and out', is much less fuss

If the Tram's in the station, do you rush, or play it cool?
You want to get on, but don't want to be the fool
Who displayed their urgency, only to be denied
As the doors slam shut, an automated broadside

And then if you get on, do you rush for a seat?
A Priority Chair, so you can rest your feet
Then put your bag on the other seat, hoping to deter
A fellow traveller, from resting their rear

Then out comes the phone, a link to your ranks
Whilst you're locked in this tube with your fellow Mancs
Standing in circles around a yellow pole
Holding your breath to avoid catching a cold

At a stop, the doors open, The 'Met-Feds' are in line
"Tickets and Passes please", else you'll get a fine
2 or 3 bail out like greyhounds at Bellevue
Hilarious to see, there's always a few

The different moods that are on display
Moulded by the purpose of their journey today
The resignation of the Workforce on the morning crush
The indifference of the Off-Peakers, who don't have to rush

The exhaustion of the Day-Shift, their money earned
The anticipation of the Night-Outers with candles to burn
The intoxication of the Last-Trammers, at the end of play
The Driver who observes this ritual every day

Pressing the button whilst you are approaching
To me it seems risky, if the Tram is still moving
That awkward moment when the doors first open
And there's a crowd on the platform, waiting to get on

Then I'm off...
And I Tap Out...

As a commuter sprints towards an already closing door
An impossible distance over the platform floor
The Tram beeps a mocking song, as if to say
'You're not getting this Tram, have a nice day.'

The Storm

As I lie in bed the house creaks and groans
It's primary purpose now shelter, not home
The structure stands fast as it's drenched by rain
An indiscriminate assault by a hurricane

This storm might breach our feeble defences
As they resist the gales that relentlessly
Rattle the roof tiles, windows and fences
As Nature threatens my family

A force that just cannot be mitigated
Trees protest, some are devastated
The noise resembles a speeding train
Screaming whistled threats as the windows strain

The timbers creak, as again they're tested
"If that chimney blows over, it'll come through the roof"
A terrifying onslaught, that cannot be resisted
The power of nature if you needed proof

The aftermath as the winds recede
Branches and twigs, bins overturned
Roof tiles and fence panels to be repaired
Wherever they went, the birds have returned.

Haunted

Living a life,
My family alongside,
Much to my relief.

My loving wife,
My beautiful bride,
I don't understand her grief.

This place, I reside,
I carry on, just so,
With my family there.

They understand,
But I don't know,
I'm totally unaware.

Killed, or died,
Or maybe neither,
Maybe that would be a blessing.

This hell of dementia,
A younger me would choose either,
To stop my family stressing.

The truth be known,
I exist in my world,
Believing I'm alive.

My spirit and character,
Have long since passed,
My body is all that survives.

Marmite

A German scientist experimented
With Brewer's Yeast that he'd fermented
And if Justus von Liebig was right...
The result, it would seem
A dark ambrosial cream
A food of the Gods, Marmite.

Tom O'Connor, a Television host
Liked it spread... nice and thin on his toast
It's favoured by 'Vegies' and Vegans
It helps you work out if you want to stay thin
It's good for your eyes and good for your skin
And it cures hung over Sri Lankans.

It doesn't 'go off', Though some may scoff
It's like honey but for a savoury palate
A bite, it can prevent, As an insect repellent
Because bugs and mosquitos don't like it.

It's not propaganda, About Bill Nighy and Canada
He was caught smuggling Marmite through Customs
You see, in Canada it's illegal
Due to ingredients deemed confidential
Which left poor Bill in the doldrums.

It looks like tar
In its distinctive, dark jar
That looks a bit like Smelling Salts
So get a knife and delve
Into a jar full of vitamin b12
Some love it, but some it revolts.

The Walk-In Centre Waiting Room

I instinctively look up,
As I hear your voice,
Aggressive tones,
The language, choice,
Sat in the NHS Walk in Centre,
I cringe, as I realise,
Whilst I watch you enter,
The chairs, ...
There are spares, next to me,
Although I don't know you,
And there are others free,
Why do I know...
You will sit next to me?

The smell of weed,
Betrays your attitude,
To society, the law and your work aptitude.
Swearing with your child,
Sat on your knee,
I know that soon,
You will talk to me,
Swearing to God that you'll "*Go all out*",
Bouncing your legs,
Why do you shout?

You just can't stop talking,
You can't sit still.
Why are you here?
You're clearly not ill.

"ARRRRGH!... E'yar, did y'ear dat?"
Your clicking shoulder used to start our chat,
Boring the room about the horses you chose,
How can you sit there, picking your nose?

Why... do you seem to believe,
That the rest of the room are so intrigued,
You don't notice the contempt,
Or worse, you ignore it,
You seem to believe we appreciate your crude wit,
And why on earth would you think I'm interested,
In the fiver each way, that you have 'invested',
"9/2 odds, is that like 3/1?"
Our conversation, will go on and on,
The 330 at Kempton, you watch on your phone,
You've backed 6 and 3, Number 3's nearly home,
The final furlong, as number 8 comes in,
'Unlucky mate', but I'm glad you don't win.

Your frustration directed to the child on your lap,
Impatience and aggression, poor little chap,
Your response to his continued neglected whinge,
'Parental intervention', sees the whole room cringe.

A young child, aged 5, sits with her Dad,
Her life, so different to that of your lad,
Distracted, her apple, rolls onto the floor,
She stares, intrigued, by your behaviour,
The apple, recovered and wiped by her father,
She just... watches you, fascinated... like a child in a zoo.

139

Ghosts of my Past

Recollections of the things I did
Places where I went
People who I hung out with
Memories of the time we spent...

On pastimes, like Cubs and Scouts
School holidays, rides on bikes
Street corners where we messed about
Camping trips and Holcolme hikes

'Big' school, different ways, new friends
School days, a cross country run
A new stage starts as the last one ends
The team we played for, the trophies we won

A chance at 'The Offy' to get some cans
Or 'chip in' for a flagon of cider
A ghetto blaster playing Telekon tunes
A football 'Twenty-a-sider'

The times that we were chased by the police
Jumping fences onto Chaddy fields
Managing to keep your dinner ticket
Tomorrow, a free school meal

I think of you, some memories fade
Any issues, long since forgotten
Images of faces from past decades
People, who have long since moved on

First job, and with it, a chance to earn
Many names I don't recall
New people and new rules to learn
I wonder what became of you all

There was a day, though none of us knew
When we were together for the last time
I can't remember when I last spoke to you
We are now all past our prime

Whenever I now pass through the places
Where we met up and talked
I remember, your voices and faces
On the streets, where we once walked

Over the years, our lives have changed
Shared interests, no longer important
We've all grown older, now middle aged
But our ghosts still walk the same pavements.

Customer Services

Due to a period of unusually high demand
my call has been added to a queue
This period's lasted for around six years
And it takes ages to get through

Every call, whenever made
takes ages to be answered
A high number of calls or too few staff?
This situation has now become standard

Your staffing levels, or lack of them
Are a problem caused by Management
To make it worse, that music you play
Can hardly be considered entertainment

But I have to listen, as it repeats on loop
Over and over again
A 45-minute rendition of Greensleeves
Driving me insane

And I know that you'll answer the very moment
If I move the phone away from my ear
So I have to keep listening, to this bloody tune,
Else start all over, that's my fear

As I wait on hold, becoming increasingly irritated
I've moved up to second in line
And then you answer, "I'm sorry for your wait"
Does that make everything fine?

And as we talk, it's clear to me
The main function you perform
Is to fob me off and stop me getting
whatever I phoned you for.

Then as we part, and the call disconnects
I voice my insults and dispair
An hour of my life, that I'll never get back
Your Customer Service is more like warfare.

Thunder

Sky darkened
Pressure deepening
Clouds, blackened
Heavens opening
Thunderous crashes
Static tensions
Blinding flashes
Elec-xplosions
Bolts of lightning
Petrifying
Thunder bolts
Pet terrifying
One billion volts
Cum-nimbus lighting
Strikes and jolts
Senses, heightening
Torrential torrents
And static surging
Grounded currents
Ionising
In streaks and sheets
Electrifying
Drenching streets
Awe inspiring
Showcased for over
A Kilowatt-hour
A demonstration of the
Apocalyptic power
Of Nature... awakened.

My Boots

It's not often I go walking on a rainy day
Tempting fate, it's fair to say
Partway round, the truth I speak
It seems my boots have sprung a leak.

I can't take them off to see what's gone wrong
Else, I'm sure, I won't get them back on
My socks are soggy, my toes are wet
High technology boots, I now regret.

I'll make tracks for home, trudging through the mud
My glasses keep getting knocked off by my hood
My hands are stone cold and there's nowt to see
Can't wait to get home to a cup of tea.

I'll wash off the mud, then stuff them with paper
Put them in the cupboard, they'll dry off by later
I should get some new ones, but we go back a long way
I reckon they'll be alright on a drier day.

Resting, but elsewhere

A place I go, gradually, unwillingly,
Suddenly, immersed,
No recollection of any journey,
When? I don't know...
Now? Years ago? Next month?
I have no option,
I cannot leave,
I'm just there, as it happens,
As it happens,
If I'm not here, then I am often 'there',
Sometimes with you,
Often without,
Tossing, turning, snoring,
So out of context to my life,
I ask no questions to establish
Why I am in a newsagents?
Why I'm a fireman?
Why I am driving a bus?
Why I'm with a schoolfriend from 45 years ago?
And who are they anyway?
Why I'm driving a car I sold 12 years ago?
Crashed into by a mobile Trainer of
Confectionary creation...
What prompted my mind to invent a horrific ankle infection?
Even I don't question these...
Improbable situations,
The insurmountable problems,
The absent solutions, seemingly impossible,
But at the time, vivid, normal,
Accepted challenges, the problems so real,

Then...

Briefly, as I turn,
A taste of semi consciousness,
Almost like a theatrical interval,
Briefly understanding... I'm dreaming,
Before the Safety Curtain suddenly raises once more,
Unprepared, I'm right back into the performance,
The Second Act, Scene One,
More characters, performing,
Conspiring with my oblivious mind,
With me as the ever-present lead role,
The script and casting credited to my subconscious
consciousness,
Part of me aware that I am dreaming,
As my illogical plot thins,
Until... I'm lying in bed,
No applause or encore,
Stirring, gradually waking,
profusely sweating, understanding,
As my mind wakens
and shifts its focus to the tasks of the day,
Ignoring the ordeal that I've just faced,
Brief memories of the performance,
Already fading away,
Soon lost, forever,
Dismissed, as today's activities, distractions, commence,
Their meanings, messages, reasons,
lost,
With my mind, subconsciously, making notes,
For the next nocturnal odyssey.

Liability Disclaimers

Mind the gap
Please drink responsibly
Always read the label
The Management accept no liability.
Petrol is flammable

Look left, look right
Contains flash photography
When the fun stops, stop
May cause addiction, don't exceed three days
Lockers with sloping tops

Contains images of violence
Which you may find upsetting
Don't exceed the recommended dose
Cotton buds, "Don't insert in your ear"
They're for drying between your toes

Contents are hot
Danger of death
One of your five a day
May cause drowsiness, don't use machinery
Drinkaware.co.uk

Acid is corrosive
Bleach: Do not drink
Please Gamble responsibly
Vehicles and contents left at owners' own risk
Click 'PROCEED' to accept a Cookie

Gambleaware.org
Wash hands after use
Keep out of the reach of children
Peanuts may contain traces of nuts
Coffee contains caffeine

Clunk-Click every trip
Smoking causes cancer
Loud volumes may damage your hearing
Always test on an inconspicuous area
Contents are two servings

Cleaning in progress
Wet paint, Wet floor
Don't try this at home
Achtung Caution Cuidado Warning
Do not look directly at the sun

Plastic Bag
This is not a toy
avoid contact with the eyes
Keep clothing away from naked flames
Be responsible for your own lives.

Writing

What was that line, that I thought in the car?
The rhyme in my mind as I had a shower.
What were those words that I thought at the bar?
Something about a bee and a sunflower...
That I remembered last night, as I lay in my bed...
That came to mind, at work in a meeting...
What was that phrase that I had in my head?
At lunchtime whilst I was eating.
Whilst checking my money as I waited to pay...
When I was busy, putting up a shelf
Whilst we watched the football yesterday
It was quite funny, if I say so myself
But now it is gone.

As I walked through the woods
It came back again
Whilst lost in my thoughts
In the pouring rain
Though I had it, briefly
Something about a Swan
My memory fails me
The poem is gone
And now I am home
My memories are like vapour
So many distractions
Sitting here with pen and paper
Now that I finally have the time
What in God's name
Was that blasted rhyme?

Not Knot

Not a knot
it's not
It's got what a knot has got
It's tidy and tight
so I'm afraid
It's not a frayed
not knot.

Frost

Crunching under foot
shattered panes of ice
crystals of frost
coating the fields and woods
as the rising Sun, spreads its gaze
the cold, to warm
dry, to wet
crisp, to soft
temperature defined separation
between ice and thaw
stones cast across the frozen lake
temporarily held, suspended above the water
in the death row that is the penumbra of shade
waiting to eventually, suddenly, inevitably
fall, as if standing on the Gallows
already condemned, fate assured
to be lost forever in the water below
upon the arrival of light
by the hand of a solar clock executioner
a celestial minute hand, ticking
sweeping across the land
as a natural sundial
marking time
unrivalled precision
white turns green
steam, briefly rises from a thawing branch
before disappearing
condensing

into the tears of perished formations
drizzling the ground below
where a song thrush
forages snails under the hedgerow
unseen,
unwitnessed,
unmourned...
a stone
silently sinks to the bottom of a lake
relinquished by the frost
forever lost.

Freezing

As the temperature drops in the darkest hour
Mist forms, on grasses and flowers
The winter chills crafts new ornaments
A unique jewel formed by the elements

Temporary decorations, born and adorn
The exposed tips of leaves and lawn
Such beauty and symmetry, unnoticed so often
As the icy footpaths demand my attention

Then sunshine burns across the sky
As the dawn chorus greets the start of the day
Exposed points start to thaw
The crystal masterpieces melt away.

Fifty Plus

Middle-aged and overweight,
My jeans are too tight,
I need a change of lifestyle,

The cheese and wine,
Have had their time,
It stops now... At least for a while.

Lazy and weak,
My future bleak,
Blood pressure through the roof.

My food preferences don't help,
There's no broccoli or kelp,
It's beer and pizza, that's the truth.

I need to get out,
And move about,
And establish an exercise regime,

Time is an issue,
My size, too much tissue,
My jeans are bursting at the seam.

Daffodils

Once the Snowdrops
have announced Winter's end,
the bulbs resting beneath the moss,
awaken, to send stems towards the skies,
pushing through the frost.

The Swifts and Swallows are yet to depart
their homes in sunnier climes,
the daffodils already announce,
the arrival of warmer times.

An early reward for eager bees,
nectar to nourish a hive,
a reliable source, for a dependent bug,
struggling to survive.

As the sun casts rays, low and long,
yellow flames ignite the lane,
their trumpets blast Amarillo song,
to welcome Spring again.

Spring pushes through, new life begins,
the end of Winter chills,
leaves on trees and baby birds,
'A host of golden daffodils.'

As the sun grows stronger and
takes a place, higher in the sky,
the April showers force them down,
the start of their demise.

Bluebells, tulips and lavender thrives,
Summer's floral display brings cheer,
the daffodils recede, as May arrives,
they will rest until next year.

The daffodil, rebirth, optimism,
as nature starts to sing,
a Lenten Lilly, loved by my Mum,
a joy, that returns each Spring.

(Love you Mum)

Being

There is a thing,
That I have,
A thing... that is mine,
A thing that only I know,
Or... I think I know it...
At least, better than anyone,
Though I don't fully know it,
Nobody can see it, touch it or take it.
It just is, what it is,
I think I now understand it,
I accept it now, as it is,
And despite its flaws,
It means no harm to *any* other,
For all its unintended secrets,
The things hidden, so deeply, even from me,
Hidden, or yet to be discovered?
Will I ever know it all?
Character, preferences,
The depth and complexity,
The insecurities, the dependencies,
The joys and the sadness,
The regrets... the darkness,
The pride and the shame,
My confidence and emotions,
Values and loves, expressions and intuition,
My reactions, fears,
My spirit and soul,
This, 'thing', is me.

Hello,

If you have made it this far and are reading this page, then I assume that you have read at least some of my poems.

I hope that you didn't find the police experiences too serious or depressing.

I'd like to think any colleagues reading this book might be able to relate to the incidents I have relied on and would maybe recognise the process that is in part, my way of dealing with my experiences, which were, all too often, serious and depressing.

The animal and environmental poems are difficult.
I feel such compassion towards animals and nature. It is difficult to see such cruelty, especially in the pursuit of entertainment.
Man is such a cruel creature.

I don't quite know where this poetry thing is leading but would welcome any feedback or comments.

I particularly welcome any endorsements that I might be able to use in a Second Edition, should there be one.

If you feel inclined, please contact me.

Many thanks,

Richard.

jre6198@gmail.com

JeffersonPoetry.co.uk

@jre6198

The Police Treatment Centres
https://www.thepolicetreatmentcentres.org/fundraising/donating

Care of Police Survivors
https://ukcops.org/

Samaritans
https://www.samaritans.org/donate-now/

The League Against Cruel Sports
https://www.league.org.uk/Pages/Category/how-to-donate

People's Trust for Endangered Species
https://ptes.org/ways-to-give/

The Soi Dog Foundation
https://www.soidog.org/content/make-donation

Bleakholt Animal Sanctuary
https://www.bleakholt.org/ways-to-help/

Hollins Vale Conservation Group
https://gf.me/u/ytt8u2

The Royal British Legion
https://www.britishlegion.org.uk/